My Yearning Never Ends

Illusions of A Dream

The Sequel To:
Tears of An Empty Heart

Antonio Fleming

Iqra Publishing Inc

Copyright © 2020
Antonio Fleming
My Yearning Never Ends
Illusions of A Dream
All rights reserved.

No part of this publication may be reproduced, distributed, or transmitted in any form or by any means, including photocopying,
recording, or other electronic or mechanical methods, without the prior written permission of Iqra Publishing Inc., except in the case of brief quotations embodied in critical reviews and certain other noncommercial uses permitted by copyright law.

Antonio Fleming

Printed in the United States of America
First Printing 2020
First Edition 2020
ISBN: 978-1-7330041-9-0

10 9 8 7 6 5 4 3 2 1

Sale of this book without the front cover may be unauthorized. If this book is without cover, it may have been reported to the distributor as
"unsold or destroyed" and neither the author nor distributor may have received payment for it.

Published & Distributed by:
Iqra Publishing Inc.
157 Sunset Avenue
Atlanta, GA 30314
www.iqrapublishing.com
Edited by Chief Editor: Lori McCaskill of the IPI team.

IN THE NAME OF
GOD
THE COMPASSIONATE, THE ALL MERCIFUL

All praise and thanks are due to Allah ta'ala alone, the Sustainer and Creator of existence. May the choicest blessings and peace be upon the last of the righteous messengers and prophets,

Muhammad ﷺ his family, Companions and all those who follow in his footsteps till the blowing of the trumpet.

قلْ إنَّمَا أنَا بشَرٌ مِثْلُكُمْ يوحَى إلَيَّ أنَّمَا إلهُكُمْ إلهٌ وَاحِدٌ فَمَن كَانَ يَرْجُو لِقَاءَ رَبِّهِ فَلْيَعْمَلْ عَمَلاً صَالِحاً وَلَا يشْرِكْ بِعِبَادَةِ رَبِّهِ أَحَداا ﴿١١٠﴾

Say: "I am only a human being like you. It is revealed to me that your God is One God, therefore whoever wishes to reach Allah (before death) let him do improving deeds (the soul's cleansing) and let him not associate anyone with Him in the worship of his Lord".

(Surah Al-Kahf: 110)

Dedication

I thank Allah ta'ala for bestowing upon me the creative gift of being able to detail my thoughts and dreams so passionately. I thank Him for granting me the ability to discover love, understand how to love, and the heart of appreciating the privilege it is to love. Love is not an illusion, nor is it lost in the days of our ancestors. I'm thankful for every woman Allah ta'ala bestowed upon my life in which He taught me the value of love. I also thank Allah ta'ala for awakening me to be a man, one who knows not to take love for granted and whose not afraid to open his heart to love.

Table of Contents

"I'm Sorry" 1
"Maybe I Miss" 4
"In My Soul" 7
"The Sun" 9
"Mystic Angel With Butterfly Wings" 13
"One Million Times" 17
"Yearning" 22
"Sometimes" 26
"Are You Living" 31
"When I" 35
"Fault Me" 39
"What Am I To Do" 43
"Compelled" 46
"I Do Not Cry" 49
"Vulnerable Heart" 51
"Hummingbird" 53
"By far" 58
"If I Never" 62
"Am I Wrong" 64
"Why Should I Awaken" 68
"Realized" 71
"Sacrifice" 73
"If I Were" 76
"If You Cry In The Dark" 78
"You Are" 80
"Believe I'm In Love" 82
"Unfortunate" 85
"Slave Puppet" 88
"Taste" 91
"I am" 93

"I'm Sorry"

As I face my broken reflections in the silence
    surrounding my existence
    I find understanding and self-elevation
by the acknowledgement of yesterday's ignorance
    My selfishness caused me to fail at achieving your acceptance
    because I was traveling to a destination with no arrival.

Precious, by heart I'm sorry beyond mere spoken words
    for guiding you nowhere in our togetherness
    beyond the intimacy of selfish desires
I'm sorry for constructing a life of ignorance for myself
    and disrespecting the rare breath of life you are
    by embracing your essence with my broken attributes
I'm sorry for allowing you to witness me journeying as a lost child
    with no sense of balance or purpose
    an existence with definition greatly undefined
I'm sorry for hiding from you and using your genuine affection to overshadow the fact:
    I have no true understanding of myself.

I'm sorry for constantly making you feel undesired, unappreciated,
    and meaningless

to a closeness you comforted with your captivating warmth
I'm sorry for diluting the expectations you envisioned of us
    for embedding your life with regretful tears
    on account of my stupidity
    and the elements of no sustainment
I'm sorry for cheating on you
    and for trying to make you feel insecure as though I was pure
I'm sorry for lying to you concerning the inner depths of my emotions
    even the conflicts of life we faced
    because if I honestly loved you as I cry
    instead of withering as an un-nurtured fool
    I would have not only cherished the irreplaceable light you are
    but I would have unquestionably
    solidified our togetherness with no elements of fear suppressing my steps.

I'm sorry for lowering my standards and walking out of your life
    only to sit alone chasing memories and staring at your pictures in the dark
My fallen love
    I'm sorry in true sincerity
    for I am not just seeking your forgiveness
    but the forgiveness of God as well
    for disrespecting your honor
    acting as though you're replaceable when you are not.

I was blessed by His will
    with the ability of discovering how magnificent you are
    and my offering of gratitude in return
    was a development of emptiness and lack of gratitude
As a fallen creation I may lay void of your acceptance
    but always know that my soul cries openly
    for the immeasurable beauty of your smile
You are the element suspended within my existence
    that makes my life significant and complete
No dream can replace the exotic sweetness of your breath
    I'm sorry for standing before you less than a man
    hurting you instead of loving you
I'm sorry for breathing before you as a boy
    When I was groomed by a Queen to be a King.
I'm sorry!

"Maybe I Miss"

Maybe I render too much of myself
To the illusions I dream
Because it's comforting to believe
I'm blessed enough to be thought of by you.

Maybe my emotions are sensitive
Given
I've forgotten my last erotic touch
Or just rebelling against Cupid's puncturing my heart
And allowing me to breathe
Without anyone to love.

Then again
Maybe I just miss you enough
To desire not the knowledge of knowing
What it feels like to lose your thought
Or discover sensation uncentered upon you.

Maybe I miss you enough
To stand before you
As an immortal Gardenia
Given the chance
To choose not to journey upon selfishness
That causes your warmth to feel unappreciated or
disrespected as a woman.

Maybe I miss you enough
To follow no footsteps of your priors
Enough
To lay my desires behind the walls of no lies
Nor fear conveying what's stirred inside
Even If
I'm secretly rejected, doubted, or unheard
Given what we both know is true
'That No More Than Open Words Have We Shared.'

Maybe I miss you enough
To cherish greater than the irreplaceable acceptance
You are offering
Enough
To recognize a once in a lifetime blessing
Only granted by God's mercy.

Regardless
Of what's classified as enough
I am not afraid to prove
'I Miss You'
Or foolish enough to portray
I am significant without your smile.

The tears of my yearning
Descend upon the seal of my loneliness
Puncturing its tenderness
With passion so intense and rich with meaning
That a single drop
Would extinguish the flames of the soul.

I Miss You, Beautiful
And even if I force myself to love in your absence
Truthfully my heart will never stop loving you.

"In My Soul"

In peace I lay
Before the mental capturing of your presence
    within a dream
Sensuous fragrance of you, I enhance
Stimulating reason for me to journey
Upon your priceless treasure
'I Burn with Silent Temptation'
Eliminating the darkness settling between the pillars of my
    fibers
I ignite the stem of a scented candle
By the fire dwelling in my soul for your smile
'Elements of Infinite Love'
Upon witnessing the profound beauty of your creation
A life diamond of my flaws
Breathless I internally become
As I shake outlining the softness of your lips
With the inner veins of my heart
Euphoric sensation I bask in
From the connection of your essence
Breathing upon my flesh
How I dream of being the water you desire
Or lost in your ambiance
Transfixed I lay within my endeavors
Vulnerable mentally and emotionally
As I trace into the center of your back
'The Replica of Your Breathless Smile'

With the moisture of my tongue
A rare rose known to life as:
'IRRESISTIBLE'
The taste of you is beyond exotic
Yet small fragments of your sweetness
Give me the impression you bathe with yellow dragon fruit
As I bypass the given taste of you
I remove the core of my heart
And place it on the pillow beside you
'So Beautiful You Are'
Enchantingly I whisper into your ear
What's detailed in the depths of my SOUL…

"The Sun"

Silently I yearn to walk beneath the eye of heaven

    with my wings expanded

Revealing the warmth I cherish internally

    is not empty words

Pure affection stifled by the cancerous

    loneliness in the fibers of my heart.

Never did I imagine

    crawling for an angel's affection

Would blanket my hollowness

    with tears that create shadows.

Sometimes I feel as though

    I'm pinioned as fowl

Restricted, not pruned

    for my passion is mysteriously arrested

    holding you is a fantasy

    and breathing you in

Is a dream I can't unyoke myself from.

Missing the dream you are

    may keep me staring at illusions of you in the dark

    and yearning to taste your whispers in the rain

Yet no matter how time hides me

    suspending an embrace

    I'd crawl naked across the Sierra without water to refresh

You will always be everything

    I would fall to my knees for.

A seraph

    in the physical form of an oriental lily.

"If" I am ever forgotten

    remember me by a word

Nothing which constitutes who I am as a whole

Solely a distinguishment of what you are

"BEAUTIFUL!"

My celestial bliss...

  My Red Diamond...

    My Palos Verses Blue...

Within my dreams

    I am your pillow

    your Spartan

    your halo

Yet, I yearn to walk under the solar disk

    as a reflection of life's most precious jewel

Your Smile

"Mystic Angel With Butterfly Wings"

Mystic angel with butterfly wings

Where have you drifted to?

Will the magnificent glare of your reflection

    ever embellish my retinas again

    or am I destined

    to exist upon broken fantasies

Infinitely crawling through illusions with

    no destination?

Where have you drifted to?

Internally mirrored as a clogging spring

    for today feels like every yesterday

My footsteps have distinguished

    the essence of a myth in your atmosphere

Unworthy of breathing

Where have you drifted to?

The sun resembles the moon to me

    whereas, time seems to shelter my shadow

    in a magnified eclipse

  . of penetrating regrets and loneliness

How I yearn to be free of empty dreams

    and empty moments of silence

Life's blessing of my passion

    I miss you.

Beyond timid cries of spoken words

    which seemingly drift aimlessly

    as a dandelion in the wind

No secret is my thirst.

I lay at my window combing delusions

    because I need to feel your heart pulsating

    as your finger tips channel upon the whiskers of my flesh

I need to taste

    the hidden nectar of your sweetness

Even if it's no more voluminous than an atomic measure of your breath

    I need to witness your smile.

Angel with butterfly wings

Where have you drifted to?

Emptiness

    may send invisible arrows into my heart

For blind I have become to life outside of a dream

    yet no matter the silence that strangles me

Forgetting you is not an option.

Mystic Angel with butterfly wings

    the blood of my heart belongs to you.

"One Million Times"

One million times a day

    my yearning blows kisses to the essence of you

Given,

    I am unable to lay dove feathers

    beneath the preciousness of your perfection.

One million times

    my tongue engraves the mirage of your silhouette

Within the wind stream

    while seductively

The falling tears puddling in my heart

    call out to you in my sleep.

One million times

I stand by myself in the silence

Enveloped as a slave by loneliness

Secretly,

    I embrace the unseen rafters of life

Delusionally holding the blessing of you in my arms

    so delicate and soft you are.

One million times

    I caress the hollow gentleness of my face

    with the tip of my fingers

While selfishly imaging

    it's the soft irresistible seduction of your touch.

One million times

    my reflection is stared upon in a mirror

    and I make believe

That I can see you

    walking in the shadows of my soul.

I yearn with pure sincerity

    to kiss your heart

I inhale and exhale

    for no reason other than to love you.

One million times

    I daydream

While dreaming within a dream

    of teasingly biting your hidden lips

Feeling your heartbeat by holding your hand

    more so,

Of swallowing the air you breathe.

When I think of you

I feel your footsteps tiptoeing in my heart.

One million times a day
    a waterfall of tears descends in my soul
While the bare flesh of my knees mend with the earth
    for all I seek
Is to prove I love you beyond words.

There is no significance without you!

One million times a day
    I paint you a replica of your grace in the wind
    and blow kisses to who you are upon my knees
One million times
    I embrace my wrong and strive to be better
    because I'd rather die than to break your heart

I love you!

"Yearning"

If there was some way

    I could suppress the yearning for you

    or escape the despair

    of resting my head on a pillow of dried tears

Maybe my heart wouldn't feel like a fallen Mauritius feather

    in the window of hidden time.

How I wish,

    I could close the shades of my eyes

    and open them to the sweetness of your embrace

Or the mesmerizing beauty of your smile

    sculptured in a Juliet rose

    which was molded on the buds of my tongue

    whereupon no matter how far we are bridged apart

The nectar of your essence I'd taste.

Whether it's deemed in the moon's fluorescence

    on a starlit night

Or within the spiraling of the morning star

    one could witness by gazing into my eyes

That I'm losing perspective of myself

    being non-existent in your time and space continuum.

I try to dream

    to elude the emptiness growing

    and subside the pain of being alone

    yet, I just keep envisioning myself crawling to you

Gracefully

    as a puppet with no strings

Only for the essence of your grace to fade

    each time I'm a breath away from your touch.

I wish my distant flower

    that I could reach beyond the darkness of my shadow

For the soft texture of your lips

    or that you had the ability to translate

The passage I've scrawled upon my chest

    with dry glass for you.

"Infinite" is my love"

If only I didn't have to dream

    of being of your ambiance

I'd dissect my heart

    and place its matter beneath your feet

No longer having to yearn in tears

    of proving I love you.

Truly my love

    is greater than a fairytale.

"Sometimes"

Sometimes

Just holding the outer casing of my pillow

    is not enough to subside the pain

    of being a distant thought to you

A lingering image that comes and goes

    as a quetzal.

Rare diamond of my dream

    I need to witness the reflection of myself

    in the gateway of your eyes

I need to know beyond selfish delusions

    and dreams that suspend me in memories of yesterday

    that for one micro moment of life

I'm sincerely thought of by you.

Fantasies of a sheltered dream

    are all I see

When I'm able to conjure the strength

    to stare out my window

Searching for your irreplaceable smile

    my yearning now is not to be here.

I dream of tasting your internal oxygen

    being the blanket of your embrace

I dream of being thought of by you

    for this feeling of being unknown to you

    is as enduring as an illusional forehead kiss

For it causes the blood

    of my inner yearning

    to replicate a rain forest

Within the chambers of my heart

    the precious rose of you lays.

Cold sweat

    propelled from loneliness gild my oasis

As I toss-n-turn in the night's glow

    reaching out to images of your grace

My heart breaks not to be there.

Beautiful,

    I need to feel you in my arms

    so intensely, your aura I thirst for

I'd crawl upon broken glass

    just to hear the softness of your whispers

    or merely to inhale your essence

Even if I'm not thought of by you.

So lost I am within myself

    facing the mirror of reality

Standing as a forgotten foreign thought to you.

For one moment

    just one moment of time

I need to believe beyond all other things

    that at some unexpected point

Within the complexity of your thoughts I exist.

You are breath

    Vision!

    Desire!

      Life is you and so immeasurable you are.

As a ghost I may walk before your eyes

    existing with no shadow

Yet there's nothing I wouldn't give

    to gaze upon the sun

    knowing I'm thought of by you

Even if its measure is

    the blinking of an eye.

"Are You Living"

Are you living

    or just commonly existing within life

    as an entity who possesses nothing greater than a beautiful smile

What is your purpose for breathing

    beneath the stars

When you think of yourself in whole without dreaming

    do tears of joy fall within the gateway of your heart

For your internal essence applauds the extraordinary woman you are

    or does your inner weakness expand

    birthing pillars of reason you find comfort in

Psychological pleasure

    of why it's acceptable to be weak-willed

    and unloving to yourself.

What is sincerity to you

sincerity beyond mere words I seek definition as an excuse

Can you say without thought

    that you are a jewel

    the element of fulfillment

    oxygen for the soul

Have you achieved the true essence of self

    or are you completely lost of understanding

    and direction

What do you offer

    if you're subjected to extract your submissive nature

    your rights to be respected and self-peace

    for spoken words instead of what love is.

Do you believe

    the identity of you is important

    and deserves to be nurtured, respected, and appreciated

Is there any significance to your grace

    are you living

  or just commonly existing to be seen and admired
Why are you traveling through each day
  in a circle that constitutes nothing
Reaching for no more than what's granted through charity
  someone's compassion and generosity
What makes today different from yesterday?

What have you learned rising from your stumble
  and opening your eyes
Life
  so precious it is
  so beautiful
Yet it will never be discovered or explored
  when one builds their foundation upon the cinder blocks
  of self-pity, misery, and selfishness.
If the darkness can't hide
  then how can you?

I see you!

I believe in you

Rise and shine as the irreplaceable blessing you are.

"When I"

Exotic butterflies I see

    dancing above a waterfalls rush

    when I secretly envision

    the life angel you are.

When I close my eyes

I run from looking into your own

    reflecting upon unmeasured beauty my internal passion

    can only govern in a fantasy untold

When I close my eyes

I make believe I'm breathing your air

    subjecting my vulnerability to the elegant beauty of your smile

Silent cries of loneliness

    enslave my tears in the windows of time

    for I am invisible

to who you are.

Beyond the hidden gazes I've stolen subconsciously

    that have seduced my peace

    and implanted desire which seems not to fade

Upon hummingbird wings my thoughts lay cascading in a dream

    yearning to witness the light of heaven

    rise and fall

    in the shadows of your essence.

White grapes and papaya slices

    bridge your lips in my fantasies

Brazilian rose petals

    I blow to your smile in the wind

French vanilla I burn

    to illuminate the darkness of your hemisphere

If only I wasn't symbolic to a mockingbird

    nurturing your ambiance with long stem strawberries

    wouldn't be a sheltered dream.

When I close my eyes

I French kiss the wind that caresses you

    lay rose petals stolen from my heart beneath your feet

    and bathe you with my tongue at your request

When I close my eyes

I see you beyond mental fascination

    that suspends my awakening in the night

So magnificent your are

    to all that I am.

When I close my eyes

I don't just fantasize about defining my love for you before the world

    I imagine tasting your whispers with my fingers

    because outside the dreams I dream

    that allows me to hold you in the rain

    and appreciate your sensuousness with sincerity

Reality elevates my emptiness

    knowing this single moment of selfishly daydreaming

maybe all I will ever achieve

When I close my eyes

I no longer make believe you love me

I breathe within your heart you do.

"Fault Me"

In those unexpected moments your eyes find themselves
    being serenaded by the fluorescent mystery of the stars
And your arms physiologically replicate the wind
    by holding the precious warmth of yourself
The silent tears you shelter within
    can be felt descending in my soul
    as the nectar of a Balsa Blossom.

Fault not those
    who falsely offered themselves as men
    in the windows of your yesterday
Cultivating no more than seeds of stratagem
    which rooted fragments of insecurity
    in the delicate pillars of your heart
Fault not those
    who never understood self and appreciated not

the life blessing you are

Fault me

    yet I beg of you to forgive me

    for failing to be your last first kiss.

Fault not those

    whom failed to sprinkle

    black orchid petals upon you in the night's glow

Those pretenders

    who constituted childish lies

    and governed your sincerity with treachery

    just to breathe a measure of your air

Fault not those

    who existed in your ambiance with a destination of no arrival

    and offered your smile only delusions

    which merited no substance

Fault me

    for acting like a boy instead of a man

  and not cherishing your heart as God commanded

  in the very moments you bestowed upon my life your grace.

In whose hands lies my soul

  I ask that you fault me for being a reflection of everything that's beneath your worth

  yet forgive me

  for being deceitful to your footsteps

  and lacking to remind you without effort

  of how irreplaceable you are

Fault me

  for fearing the genuineness of my emotions

  and not protecting your smile

  as I was granted life too

Fault me

  for not standing beside you

  in the moments you needed a rock, a pillow,

  or your inner thirst to be fed

  from the cultivated lining of my heart.

Life Treasure, fault not those

    who wasted your time with ignorance

I ask that you fault me

    for not taking the time to learn

    the definition of love from you

But I beg of you to forgive me

    for not implementing it to you.

Please accept the sincerity of my apology

    for I was wrong to take you for granted

    and not showing by actions that you're appreciated and irreplaceable

I'm sorry....

"What Am I To Do"

What am I to do
    when I begin waking from sleep that was never
given
Enveloped in wetness
    that's derived not from the contained heat of self
    but yet drowning from the internal tears
    that descend continuously to the core of my soul
I miss you!

What am I to do
    when the silent dreams I dream
Seemingly become shattered at their origin
    and the cherished images of your adorably rare
smile
    withers
    from the development of my thoughts
Induced by toxic agitation of the mind's perception

of loneliness stirring in regret
Forgotten, you will never be
    for you are to me
    like music to an Alzheimer's patient---
indestructible
To say that I miss you is a gross understatement
    for I'm hopelessly and endlessly tortured.
What am I to do
    when I come to stand under the sun
    mentally naked of gray matter
So lost without a compass
    and the stars do not align to guide me
Emotionally thirsty
    even though I'm yoked by the fantasies of your
love.

As a slave unconsciously submitting his will
    physically and mentally
I stand as a sufficient symbol of your breath
    yet what am I to do

    when my secret of loving you is no longer a secret

    and it's confirmed, I only exist because of you.

Forever my belief in you will suspend my heart
    Forever you will govern my soul
Forever I will fight for your tranquility
    security, internal strength, integrity, and respect
    yet I can no longer shelter the sincerity of my love for you
Upon my chest I crave your name
    I miss you.

"Compelled"

Lavender and vanilla, I enhance
    when I find myself caressing the mystic waves
sketching your smile
    with the vacancy of my stare
    while suspended in a desensitized dream of
silence.

[EV] O-LU*TION
    the preciousness of your image whose origin
    is the hidden canals of my thoughts.

Sustained by fallen tears I wonder
    if you are an angel
    or the replica of a fallen star
Compelled
    are the genuine elements governing my unspoken
intentions.

I breathe
I exist
I was created
    to cherish the essence of you.

Unknown

    to the softness of your embrace
I stand seeded upon discovering
    why I'm constantly suspended in a portal of self-passion
    yet denied the pleasure
    of laying orchid petals beneath the warmth of your feet
The expansive distance between us
    can hide the desires of my existence
    and countless others
But no measure of silence
    can shackle my words
    for my heart is yoked by the breath of you
    as my sincerity aimlessly rides the wind as an arachnid.

If only I knew what love was
If only your sensuous warmth found reason in me
    worthy of your acceptance
    an empty soul I would not broadcast
    an empty soul would not walk as the living dead.

Beautiful, in truth
    you are a remarkable gem of life
    inconceivable
The flower of magnificence
  The butterfly of grace
    The definition of love

If only you could communicate with the whispers of my soul
    without thought
    you'd know how special you are
    and that it's your name cemented upon my heart.
I love you....

"I Do Not Cry"

Hidden or unseen
I do not cry
   from pain internal
   sorrow
   or pity.

I do not cry
   on account of my loneliness
My countless regrets
   or the plentiful emotional losses my soul sustains.

I do not cry
   during the whispers of the night
   or day
For selfish desires my fingers and tongue
   can't seem to delight.

I do not cry
   with emptiness's issuance of indiscrimination
   against the delicate tapestry of my heart
   as it triggers fibrillation and palpitations.
I do not cry
   for the taste of life
   beyond the silent darkness

    my peace is evicted within
The ice which guarded my identity
    has melted as tears from a cave's stalactites
Descended upon the stalagmites of my grounded integrity
    dried up like dead skin textured as loneliness
    because breathing without you
    forced me to view within myself
Where the immature reflections of a man
    are now reconciled definitively
From the blind depths of selfishness
    your artwork of yesterday has risen.

I do not cry
    to save tears
I cry solely because
    I love you the blessing God created of you.

"Vulnerable Heart"

I did not know how hollow I was
How vulnerable was the fabric of my heart
Until I stumbled upon the sensational grace of your essence
Which now sustains my blood flow.

Your smile
Is the seal etched into my vertebrae
I think of you
Because I need to know there is more to life
Than illusions, dreams of passion
I do not conquer or abuse
The life blessing that's meant to be cherished
Willingly I submit my lips to the softness of your fingertips
Guide my way to Paradise
My happiness I'd sacrifice
For you are true completeness.

My reserved thoughts of you
Beat against the phantom of my mind
As the oceans thrust against the rocks of the bay
Shallow is the portal of time that holds a day
Stolen from the realms of your grace

So many windows
To view the existence of life form
Yet only one birth is credited for the breathless beauty of an angel.

I find you to be an ice crystal
That melts not in the sun
There is not a moment given in time
I wouldn't run without the coating of my flesh
To bridge the mysteries of our hemispheres
I dream of you perching in my soul
That's why I know we should reach for eternity
Let's not grow to love
My Everything
Let's waste away together.

"Hummingbird"

If I could kiss your lips with the petal of a Lisanthus

    the burning of my hidden passion

Would merge with my yearning

    causing my tears to gravitate to your silhouette.

Illusions of a shattered fantasy

    has my heart atrophying

    awakening another day

Unyoked

    of the breathless beauty of your smile

    and the soft seductiveness of your whispers.

So cold I am in a tunnel of darkness

So lost...

So alone...

I hover at my window as a hummingbird

    peering into the fading of the horizon

Mentally fingering the plastered pictures of you

    I cherish in the grottos of my mind.

How do I cease

    the mountain of passion dripping from the essence of my breath?

When I can't escape

    even in the realms of sleep

        the portal of missing you.

As I hover about my window as a Hummingbird

    my dreams seem fractured

For time has punctured my heart

    and the pulsating emptiness

Floods the prairie of my smile.

Life's angel

    I need you more than words

Blow me a kiss into the stars

    and the aura of my heart

    will drift to your shadow.

You are the reflection of my breathing

    the Caribbean Bougainvillea painting

    mesmerizing the iris of my eyes

The overwhelming dream freezing

    my soul in time

I'd sacrifice everything that is in me

solely for you to feel yourself within my heartbeat.

I miss you!

I need you!

Without you my existence is for naught

No life.. No purpose...

Everyday

I'm unfiltered with the preciousness of your touch

The torqueing pain causes far more than

unheard whispers

To fall from the windows of my soul.

As I hover in my window as a Hummingbird

peering into the fading of the horizon

while your smile creates footsteps in my mind

All I know is I love you

and I'll die internally unable to breathe with you.

Only your acceptance makes life meaningful...

"By far"

Somewhere by far

Beneath the saunter of angels

Lingers the seduction of irreplaceable sweetness

Hidden whispers so foreign

So exotic

That paramnesia has me sitting in the night

Trying to steal atom measures of your essence from the wind.

So unknown

Exist the hypnotic softness of your touch

A passion so thirsted

I'm blanketed with selfish delusions of chasing your footsteps in the sand

Tasting the misty droplets cascading from your lips

Merely to bridge time

For I'm tired of being a mystery to your moment.

Why?

Do desires have me feeling symbolic to Birds of Paradise

A Paraselene unseen

When all I yearn for as the horizon hides my shadow

Is to breathe in your smile.

Sensation only achieved

Momentarily by the enduring of a dream.

If I employed butterflies

To carry away your inner tears

And secretly blanketed your essence in the dark

With crushed sprinkles of my marrow's fiber

Would you mind?

If I scripted upon

The greatest star in the constellation, Canis Majoris

Why I breathe to be a ventricle for your heart

    Would you mind?

Crawling to your silhouette is not a secret

If only you could walk through my shadow.

Holding you with my woven feathers

May be a fantasy

More so, feeding you chocolate dipped strawberries upon the shore

No matter how raindrops fall between our exhales

Your happiness I crave to explore.

Reach to me as Psyche before your sexual awakening

And I'll climb all obstacles to be your Cupid

Your last first kiss is what I breathe for.

Grant me one chance to feed your smile and my sincerity

Will elevate the comfort of your pillow

I only inhale

To walk as your slave

I belong to you.

"If I Never"

If I never fall to my knees while asking God
    for your protection
    and comfort
Assurance would never hold me
    surrounded by peace in the dark.

If I never feel that I've failed
    nor have become forgotten by your desire
Just as the moments I cherish our yesterday's
    then the dream I shadow myself within
    is powerless to eliminate my constant suffering
    for I have you not to hold
    and I would bleed without meaning.

If I never face my reflection
    beyond the invisible shadow cast in my mirror
    then I'll never witness in truth who I am
    understand my worth
    nor ever accept that I need to outgrow childish endeavors
And I'll never offer you anything greater
    than the replicated footsteps of those who failed you
before.

'Hurting You Is Not An Obstacle!'

Second chances

    aren't always given to make a first impression
    and knowing my love for you
    is beyond the mere understanding of life
I refuse to stand as a fool
    denied the taste of your warmth.

My love
    I'll never stop swimming
    through the unstable concrete of temptation
    to hold your hand
Until my soul
    has definition within your thoughts
    and I am given life to lay petals beneath your feet.

"Am I Wrong"

I stand penetrated by darts of the sun
Captured by the butterfly's graceful motion in flight
Droplets of the cloud's mist
Hydrate the seeds of my thoughts.

Am I wrong?
Intensely I wonder
Sincere are my intentions
Yet am I wrong?
Wrong to walk by far
Unknown and unheard
Selfishly believing
The gems in your eyes
Have yet to lust
A by-product of your true potential.

Am I wrong
To envision the clarity of your smile
When I linger on life and its meaning
Yet know within myself
Without knowing of you
That it has yet to reach the pinnacle of its beauty
Nothing being given from yesterday.

Am I wrong
In asking you to rise not as a Queen
For her heart of soul is merely a pawn
Royalty with no authority
Rise I ask
Through the silence of time
Significant and immeasurable
As the woman God gave you life to be.

Am I wrong
To fall upon my knees
Asking that peace govern you
Greater knowledge befall you
Embodied strength comfort you
And that you level the field of your heart to sprout insecurities
Which cause you to doubt the lily you are.

Truly I hope I am not wrong!

The word
May have ruled upon your steps
Yet your words are freedom and power
Never can your mind be contained
Only you can surrender to believing in how special you are
Beyond yesterday.

"Self-Pitied Perception, I Pray You Never Embrace"

I know you are strength untold.
You are sensation unbridled.
Whether I think of you aloud or silently
My hidden intention
Is the sincerity of you
Not about fulfilling a cherished dream
I may secretly burn of in the dark
As I search the silence
For a fallen star to wish upon.

A dream
That one day allows me the internal joy
Of feeding you white grapes and Sea Urchins
On the shores of Talamone
A dream
That one day allows me
To walk in the channels of your thoughts
As we journey above the clouds
Anticipating the wonder of our destination
A dream
That one day allows me
To hold you in my arms tricking the illusion
To know of you beyond the essence of thought
And the pleasure of bowing with sincerity

Wholeheartedly thanking God
For blessing me with being your last first kiss.

It's solely about you
And only you rising to be the woman you are
Shining
Beyond the sparkle of a diamond
It's all about you.

"Why Should I Awaken"

I've adjusted my heart
But if I can't endure the dreams that I dream
Then what is the valid point in opening my eyes
Witnessing objects and creation
That measures not the life of you.

Why should I awaken from a dream
When I can lay alone and infinitely envision
Tasting the moisture your hidden nectar left upon my lips
Or searching the sensitiveness of your neck with seductive nibbles
For it is the quest of my yearning
To intertwine the cravings of my desire
With the fabric of your softness.

Why should I awaken from a dream
That allows me to whisper
Secretly to your silence
'I Love You'
Only to face reality alone and void of the air you breathe.
The illusions I birth within my dreams
Allow me to walk the streets of Jannah
Lost with no destination without you

My illusions
Teach me how to be greater than the man you seek
My illusions
Grant me what opening my eyes does not
The blissful pleasure of representing your smile within the sun.

Why should I awaken from a dream
Only to achieve
A lifetime void of the shared moments we bridged when my eyes are closed
What stirs in the depths of my soul
Should never walk within the light
Hidden.

I don't want to travel without a sense of arrival
I don't want to exist
As an entity that renders no thought within you
I want to fight the seconds of life and temptation
For your peace, respect, and definitely your worth.

Why should I awaken from a dream
That suspends my breath
Yet defines me not as the definition of your happiness
I want the opportunity to prove
I will not fail your acceptance

Set my soul free
Why should I awaken from a dream
If I belong not to you.

Until I am empty no more
I shall lay dreaming of you.

"Realized"

It was not the empty steps of my past
    that warranted me with the self-will
    to reach for greater life substance
Than mere street dreams
    and the attention of individuals
    who offered my growth no meaning
Beyond their selfishness and greed.

It was not the broken reflection
    I witnessed of myself
Without excuses granting me comfort to hide my fears within
    that manifested my inner strength
Allowing me to break
    the colossal mental yoke of insecurity
    which kept my peace subdued with tears
    sheltered in fearing who I am
Wholeheartedly believing I am greater
    than a breath of unsubstantiated dogmas or principles.

It was not
    my choice of thoughts of facing life alone
    being unthought of in the dark
    with only my inner canals hearing my words
    or my inner thoughts caring

That made me appreciate the breath of a woman with sincerity
    cherishing her stare
    her purpose, her smile, her grace and her thoughts
As time hides knowledge
    in the windows of life.

It was not
    the seeds of my dreams
That gave me peace
    nor the pillows of my desires
    that nurtured me with burning passion
Your smile
    dictates the flow of blood within my heart
I grew up
    because I realized without thinking
    I offered you nothing of substance
Nothing more than disrespect
    selfishness and childish endeavors
I would rather be without life
    than to exist
    as failure to your love.

"Sacrifice"

I may stand alone as silence comforts my loneliness
    yet the genuineness of my dreams will forever center
upon you
I close my eyes
    and dance gracefully with your silhouette in the rain
    gleefully kissing every drop that falls upon your smile
I sing to you
    using no spoken words
    only placing your hand on the cotton covering my heart
I run to you when you're less than a breath away
    not to show the surrendering nature of a slave
    but to genuinely define that your fulfillment is my
sincerity
I would walk across the Arabian desert in a sand storm
    with no water to quench my thirst
    until the joints in my ankles shattered
    just to caress your softness with my fingertips once more
    even if the meaning is forever lost upon a destination
with no arrival.

I would define my true sincerity with no fear
    by fighting a Silverback in the wild
    with both hands tied behind my back
    just for you to know I regret every breath inhaled
    ungoverned with your acceptance
I would lay on the ice of the Antarctic

    imitating the awe of a seal in my nakedness
    weakening not as frost subdues me greatly
    just to inhale the sweet elegance of you
    while looking into the mystique of your eyes
Time may have extended our last mutual stare
    or even the last genuine words you acknowledged from me
    yet no matter the measure of silence
    the definition of your smile is infinitely cherished
    by the tears falling within my soul.

'Sufficient Are The Words Echoing Within My Heart'

I could be beaten in the distinguished methods of an ancient rebellious slave
    until my escaping blood depletes my oxygen
    never will I unyoke you from the fabric of my heart
My Butterfly
    even when I don't dream of your affection once given
    my internal passion burns in the flaming replica
    of a lily beneath water.

'If Only I Could Express How Deeply I Love You'
    I could spend my perpetual life
    allowing my sense of feeling to be affected by using my feet
    for I am without hands
My vision of you conceived by the sounds echoing within my canals
    absent ocular integrity

    for I am without sight
A Contortionist, I twist my body
    forced to share the suppression of my tears
    firmly biting into my bottom lip.

I would embrace these God-given attributes
    wholeheartedly in peace
Not for you to know my cries of love are honest
    nor for you to know without thought
That I would never define ignorance before you
    causing forbidden tears to trickle upon your warmth.
Rather, more so the naked truth
    'I Need The Essence of You to Complete The Man God Created Me to Be!'

"If I Were"

If I were a bird
Searching for heaven
Or the taste of life that exists beyond the R.E.M. of a dream
I'd follow your shadow into the night
Lay your hand upon my feathers
And give refuge to your smile with my wings.

If I were a flower
Thirsting for hydration
And seeded in quicksand
For the chance to earn your admiration
I'd rise
Blossoming in full effect
To reflect
The indelible beauty of you.

Deep within the recession of my thoughts
I cherish you as the essence of time
The thirst of precious
Black Gold
Non-Existent in life.
If I were the tears of paradise
I'd cry you a mystic river
Above the clouds of Eden
Bathe you and dry your softness with my tongue.

If I were the sun
I'd entice your eyes
And seduce them from infinite blindness.

If I were the wind
I'd carry you to ecstasy
And bring you the rings of Saturn
Distinguishing without thought
You are the most beautiful angel
Of all the worlds.

If I were a sacrifice
I'd extract the pain that may dwell in your heart
And surrender to its lining
The nectar of my peace
I'd bridge your discomfort with happiness that's genuine and sincere
More importantly
I'd commit to you my freedom.

If I was fortunate to be anything of God's creation
I'd be love and love you
Because you are the Omega of my heart.

"If You Cry In The Dark"

If you cry in the dark
Then allow the tears of my essence
To caress the tender fabric upon your face
Without sorrow bridging your veins
For you are a phenomenal woman
One whose grace gives life indescribable sweetness
But if you smile in the moon's arc
Then smile because weakness does not define you.

A scented vanilla candle burns in the window of life between us
Sensuously illuminating the eagerness of my anticipation
In the given instant your eyes awakened
For it is my shadow
That guards your smile upon the stars.

African Ice
Formulates in the channels of my mind
When I birth thoughts of you
Yet the echoes of my words silently spoken
Are not heard
Beyond the whispers of sincerity the angels record
Drifting above the howling and chirping of the night
Orchid petals I ask God to lay beneath your grace
Peace I summon to govern your strength.
If you cry in the dark

Then lay not in the shadows of regret
Allowing the memories of yesterday
To yoke you of dispirited breaths
Cry because the genuineness of your smile
Can never be replaced.

Cry because your woman's worth
Is a genuine reflection of water
Cry because in truth and only truth
You are the identity of life
But if you smile
Then smile not because you flutter in my thoughts as a butterfly
Smile because weakness does not define you
And solely because you are the definition of BEAUTIFUL to my existence.

Cry because God created you an irreplaceable blessing
And nothing is more meaningful than the truth.

"You Are"

You are my silent inspiration
The only desire that has manifested within my soul
You are my unseen burning passion
The life element silently intensifying the principles within my character
As water trying to extinguish a flammable liquid fire
Images of your smile suppress my inner ignorance
You are the reflection of my intuition
For I dream only of your elegance in my absence.

Priceless standards I cherish beyond cravings
Though I'm suspended in chains
And yoked by yesterday's closeness
Still you are the breath of which I breathe
'Aspects of reality, for that's not a dream'
You are my development
The C-6 of my spine
A solidified divinity casting critically amazing attributes into my existence
You are my life purpose
As a slave I endlessly strive to awaken your smile
Only your self-fulfillment strengthens my weakness with pleasure
You are the inner lining of my heart
The rose growing within its chambers
Allowing me to breathe definition

You are my sincerity
My reason
And comfort
You are the light guiding me through the darkness
The silent essence whispering into my self-emptiness
"No Estás Solo"
You are the gateway to ecstasy
The diamond centered in my eyes
The love governing my soul

You are my EVERYTHING!

"Believe I'm In Love"

Silence has shackled my smile
Yet deception has not sheltered my words
Fierce are my thoughts in the expansion of the twilight.

Should I trust you
Am I holding nothing worth cherishing
Is it all worth the constant disrespect
And the endless tears that fall
How much greater is love
When deception and lies equally measure the joy we bridge.

Unlit is the candle I hold
As my arms search the air
For a pocket of comforting peace
I whisper your name with love upon my tongue
As I stand alone in the rain
Dreaming of awakening to the tenderness of your heart.

I believe I'm in love with you
But unfortunately I won't know
Until I am able to breathe as your last first kiss.
Mystic river
My eyes birth internally
For I sincerely miss
The soft texture of your warmth
Caressing my entity in the depths of your thoughts.

Sensuous passion
I desire to taste of your acceptance
As a Jackal
Hunting to quench his longing thirst.

I believe I'm in love with you
I believe I don't exist
Unless I'm of you
I believe you are the bearer of my soul
But unfortunately I won't know
Until I am able to out measure the men
That failed to secure your heart
And define true happiness within your smile.

I miss you...
I want you...
Truly I need you...
Yet I am afraid of hurting you.

A blossomed Day Lily
I affectionately place upon the moist tenderness of your lips
Taste the life nectar
Pure sweetness
I'll never be to your life
"LIMITED"
Given the opportunity to respect you.

I believe I'm in love with you
Not because I feel you expanding across my heart
Or standing in the rafters of my soul

Sincerely
I asked God to love an irreplaceable woman
And since that very moment
He governed my vision with you.

I don't believe I'm in love with you
My Blessing, I know I am....

"Unfortunate"

Imperfection holds me not
As a root beneath the soil
My timing is just unfortunate
I crawl
So desiring to rise
Life owes me nothing
What is it like to exist without pain
Having the mere ability to smell the nectar of the earth
Without the fabric of my chest drowning in oceanic tears

What is it like being alive
I mean really alive
Recognized beyond self awareness
What is it like to touch an Angel
Void of feeling, the wind unseen but noticeable force
Caresses the texture of your precious flesh
I'm not that fortunate to know
Just fortunate to breathe as a ghost.

What is it like
Standing unyoked beneath the sun
Basking without love or purpose
I yearn to walk in the rain
Feeling as though I'm carrying you in my slippery arms.

What is it like

Journeying free of thought
Uninhabited by ignorance
And no longer oppressed by dictatorship short of God
I'm not fortunate to know
Just fortunate to breathe.

What is it like
Being assured
Beyond delusions that stagnate the mind
Causing one to find comfort
In dreaming within empty dreams
What is it like to feel
And not be considered a slave by your own thoughts
I ask
Because I know not
Just fortunate to breathe.

I know not what it feels like
To witness the essence of light
For darkness and discomfort shelter my every step
I know not what it feels like
To feed my thirst without fear
Nor to birth common affection
As the act of a smile.

I crawl
I cry
Yet I will not surrender
It has been three minutes

Since I've kissed you in a dream and held warmth greater than my own
One day
I do believe wholeheartedly
That I will be fortunate
To be greater than nothing
Blessed beyond words and a dream
To hold your hand and prove failure is not an option.

One day
I shall love you without closing my eyes.

"Slave Puppet"

If I had the supreme ability
    of governing your every moment with assurance
       that withered not in the changing of four seasons
I would surrender the origin of my essence
    submissive as a slave
As a southern puppet upon a string
    I would faithfully climb
       wire and bricks in the density of each night
Just to lay the petals
    of a Dutch Amaryllis on the pillow where your smile lays
    and carve the word 'SPECIAL'
       into the wooden floor with a tear soaked petal
Solely as a genuine reminder
    of your true distinctiveness.

If for some reason beyond your control
    you become saddened
       due to the selfishness of someone else's actions
I would extract my strength
    and mail it certified to your first fallen tear
Whereupon it would gracefully sing
    'Teach Me To Love' *(by Musiq Soulchild)*
And once learned beyond the folds of a fantasy
    I would define 'Everything' *(by Jaheim and Next)*
    for you are worth far more than all.

If unfruitful thoughts
    began within the breaths of your warmth
    causing you to feel alone
    and unappreciated
My shadow would run to you
    as a Falcon soaring in flight
    sincerely embracing the softness of your being
    with definition that's as meaningful as your own
    and guaranteed not to fade in time
I would read to your doubts
    your elements of loneliness
    and your insecurities
The true story
    'Appreciated Is Forever The Life Of You.'

If adversity arose from a destination unseen
    raising with it unbalanced characteristics
    and mental confusion that unyoked you of peace
The jewels of my knowledge
    would burn through the rubbish that separate us unknown
Destined with fierceness to fight every life element
    until the breathless beauty of your smile is sustained
My understanding would establish
    an endless bridge to comfort your every step.

If darkness sheltered you
    great or small
    my eyes would be your guiding light
If I had the supreme ability

 to govern your every moment
  with assurance that withered not in the changing of four seasons
I would surrender the origin of my essence
  as a southern puppet upon a string.

"Taste"

I taste the hypnotic sweetness of your sincerity
    when I envision kissing the softness of your lips in the snow
I even feel the gentle warmth of your fingers
    caressing the fallen tears within my heart
    whenever I linger upon the thought
'I'm Forgotten By You.'

My loneliness is not overshadowed
    as I lay hidden and alone
    in the silence of my darkness
    suspended within internal passion of which is nurtured
by my dreams
I pray for you
    in the dawn of each awakening
    and beyond the realm of the twilight
May the mercy of His love comfort your preciousness
    while significantly expanding your woman's worth.

You are a rose enveloped within a diamond
    a diamond embedded in a star
You are the essence of life in the purest form
    and I can't continue fearing what may never be
    only to hide what is
My emotions are governed
    by all that makes you who you are

'A Human Replica of an Angel.'

Whenever I hold you in the channels of my dreams
    my emptiness endures a transformation of extraction
For your acceptance
    is a blessing immeasurable by understanding
'Meaningful Defines You With No Definition'
    for special is only an attribute...

My heart may cherish the completeness of your divinity
    the essence of my soul may be guided by your integrity
As my every desire birthed
    may find genuine fulfillment in the beauty of your smile
    yet I will never feel full of life
    until your heart knows 'I Love You'
Without my emotions being viewed
    as an empty confined cry.

"I Believe In You!"

"I am"

I am a heartbeat

A vessel with no pulse

Reflected light of the Betelgeuse of Orion

Precious yet unseen

I am a cherished thought blanketed by concrete and suspended in time

A cracked mirror of suffocation

Atrophying without you.

I am lost in a room

Within the essence of my heart

Whereupon your whispers are the hidden windows

Illuminating the tears I use as my pillow

I yearn to open my eyes

To the sensuous shades of your grace

While internally tasting the nectar of your pores

Sexually seductive melodies of a selfish dream

Punctures the threads of my silence

As mental delusions of a desired touch

Strangles me slowly by fascination.

With exaggerated ghoulish movements

I crawl to the mirror of your smile

Which is hand scribed upon the gates of my soul

With stolen blood from my fingertips

Life I'd sacrifice

To escape the tormenting impressions of missing you.

I am lonely...

Empty without the dream of you

Fractures and disappointment yoke me

As time widens the canyon of a tearful embrace.

Gentle kisses of restrained passion

I blow seductively in lust of you

Yet tossed recklessly

As they fall prey to the current of the wind

As broken petals of an Ecuadorian rose.

Your footsteps tread upon my heart softly

Your smile is the inner lining of my soul

Cherished

Yet still I am a heartbeat.

A vessel with no pulse

For to me you are everything

A lifetime of dreaming could never measure

Whereas to you

I feel I am no more than a word

Invisible...

Forgotten...

My love is the earth between your feet

Even though missing you is eating away at me.

The End

"Signature Strokes"
By Saudia Halim
Calligraphy/Henna Artist
804-433-0596

Oh, Allah! If in Your knowledge, (this matter) is good for my religion, my livelihood and my affairs, immediate and in the future, then ordain it for me, make it easy for me, and bless it for me. And if in Your knowledge, (this matter) is bad for my religion, my livelihood and my affairs, immediate and in the future, then turn it away from me, and turn me away from it. And ordain for me the good wherever it may be, and make me content with it.

www.ingramcontent.com/pod-product-compliance
Lightning Source LLC
LaVergne TN
LVHW011212080426
835508LV00007B/745